My Body
My Best Friend

"A Healthy Relationship"

By Trudi Harper Hill

BALBOA.PRESS
A DIVISION OF HAY HOUSE

Balboa Press books may be ordered through booksellers, or by contacting:

Balboa Press
A Division of Hay House
1663 Liberty Drive
Bloomington, IN 47403
www.balboapress.com
844-682-1282

Print information available on the last page.

ISBN: 978-1-9822-5940-2 (sc)
ISBN: 978-1-9822-5941-9 (e)

Balboa Press rev. date: 03/24/2021

This book is dedicated to my Mother, who gave me the gift of life, and honored me, by allowing me to form inside of her body. I will always love and appreciate you, Mom, for our journey together, and so much more.

My Body
My Best Friend

"A Healthy Relationship"

Contents

Acknowledgements

I am one of countless people, who have been uplifted, and transformed by the lives of others. On my quest, to be my true cellf, I owe who I am, to so many. I have immeasurable gratitude, for Mother Father God, the Universe, Jesus, and my ancestors, "on whose shoulders I stand", all of them passed on tremendous opportunities and genetic blessings, along the way. I owe a special thank you to my #1 sheroe, my mom, Dr. Ruth V. Creary, Ph.D., my #1 hero, my stepdad, Dr. Ludlow B. Creary, M.D., M.P.H., F.A.A.F.P., and my #1 earth angel, sister Bridget C. Harper, M.A., who all financially assisted me, loved me anyways (when I was unlikeable) and stretched to understand my eccentricities, during my healing process. To my uncle Luther, uncle Clarence, and brother Terrence, who gave me unconditional love, and saw greatness in me, when I didn't see it in mycellf. To my baby brother Adam who made me feel special, my beloved 1stborn son, James, whose birth brought me back to life and encouraged me to find my purpose. To my baby boy Theodore, my sunshine, who gave me the gift of joy, and to my devoted husband and soulmate Dr. Virgil "Aqebi" Hill, Jr., who taught me one of the greatest lessons of my life, you all are my heartbeat. I am so deeply grateful , for all of the people who have loved, guided, inspired, influenced, molded, and rebuked me, took an interest in me, in big and small ways, and added to the collective good, in my life. Please allow me to name, more, of these great people. I pray that I don't forget anyone, but if I do, charge it to my head, and not my heart. T o my biological father, Gerald Harper, Ph.D., grandmothers, Willia Lou Turner, Dorothy Mae Fisher, Dora Clark, and Ruth Rebecca Riley, grandfathers Marvin Scott Fisher, and Thurlow Harper, to my extended family, the Harpers, Fishers, Pattersons, Goodrich's, Rileys, McCorveys, Taylors, Crearys, Pettys, Vasquez's, Hills, Porters, McNeair-Luciens, The Barnes family, Yaren Senoz and family, and to my friends and village, past and present, Tracey Hester and family, Leah Serrano and family, Kim Young and family, Lesley Mackey, J.D. and family, Dana Stovall Windt and family, Tammy "Assata" Harris and family, Carmen Cerda, C.P.A. and family, Paula "Aamut" Denkins and family, Sindi Graber and family, Aura Pinero, Yvonne Fischer, Rachel Ligon, Theodore Martinez, Sr., Stephanie Jas Bazuaye, Tramel Hutchinson, Ramona Buchanan, Robbin Jackson and family, Rev. LaRoy Wainwright, Jalannia Sutton, M.A., Zna Houston, Esq. and family, L'Tanya Portlock, Alisha Balthazar, Pamela Springer and the Nichiren Buddhist Community, Vicki Phenicie and the Self Realization Fellowship, Dr. Jeffre B. Rosenfeld, Dr. Robert Kirk, Dr. Randall & Gem Maxey, R.N., Dr. McIntosh & Sandra McIntosh, R.N., Della Bishop, Rsc.P., Dr. Theda Douglas & Momma Douglas, Frank & Bunny Wilson, Dr. Cecil & Ethelyn Motley, M.S., Ernesdyne Daves, E.D.D., Antonia Routt, Dr. Louis King, Jewel Diamond Taylor, Iyanla Vanzant, the West Angeles Church of God In Christ Family, Dr. Cecil L. Murray & the FAME & C.M.E.C. Family, Michael Ellison, Beverly Zackary, Coach Lemle, Dana Williams, Miss Efie, Miss Ratliff, Miss Carolina, and the Melrose Elementary School family, Bernadette Lucas, Ms. Medina, Mr. Landaverde, our AAU family, Cal Supreme, Coach Nash, Coach Al, and home school teachers, Kathleen Hickman and Tammy Mims, spiritual moms Gail Floyd and Kathy Shirley, Pac Hills and Cathedral staff, Ben Ramos, Oscar Leong, Martin Farfan, Lorena Griego, Momma Nia, Coach Middlebrooks, John Ferrante, Michael Godoy, Rose Santos, Beverly Staveley, Mike Trafecanty, Minerva Preciado, Robert Ryan, April Underwood and the Hari Krishna Community, Rev. Mataji of EagleWings of Enlightenment Center, Rev. Lynn and the Center of Light, Alexandria House, The African American Cultural Center Family, Reverend Meri Ka Ra, Erica Byrd & the KRST Unity Center of Afrakan Spiritual Science Family, William "Grasshoppa" Dowell, Dr. Wolfblade, The Madison Family, Cyrah Bianka, Kateria Knows, Heru/Luke One, Cristina Chereneta, Reverend Dr. Michael Beckwith, Rev. Greta Sesheta, Ujazi Calome, M.A., Queen Vuyisa, Queen Anuket, Judge Patricia Titus, Shanna Jacobsen, Eleanor Schneir, Mark Ridley Thomas, Lana LaMotte & Staff, Shanta Gabriel, Dr. Deepak Chopra, Boho Beautiful, Kamara Farai, Aloha Morningstar, Neville Goddard, Autumn Isenhour, The Snowden Family, Prandhara Prem, The Satori Family, Sol Flowa of Hana's Healing House, Hadiiya Barbel of Goddess Gloup, Johnny Desarmes, Areva Martin, Esq., Vickie Moran, Ph.D., Krishna Kaur, Dr. Joe Dispenza, Abraham Hicks, Dr. Sue Morter, and last but not least, THANK YOU to my body. You have never betrayed me, although I've betrayed you countless times, with toxic things and people, you patiently waited for me to go higher. Your humility and mercy inspire me.

THANK YOU FOR EVERYTHING!!!
YOU REFLECT THE GREATNESS OF GOD!!!

Like an oyster, to a pearl, that sacred incubation period that enables the pearl, to fully reach its destiny, so it is, the thoughts we keep, in the deepest recesses of our minds. If we will spend time with ourselves, and surrender to the clarion call, to co-exist respectfully with nature, our bodies will reveal the most beautiful creation..

Our True Self

Building a practical relationship, with my body, is one of the best things that I ever did. My body goes everywhere I go, it experiences everything I experience, every moment, achievement, win, every person, trauma, set back, and issue. My body is always working, tirelessly, for my good.

My body is my original ride or die!!!

When it comes to my personal happiness and wellness, there are (3) very important things that revolutionized my life. The first is that I AM responsible, for how good I feel, and what I attract into my life, by what I think, say, and do, not the devil or other people. It's not haters, family, or friends, who are responsible, for my happiness (or lack thereof), it is, simply, me. Prior to taking personal responsibility for how I felt, I was overly religious, and therefore, judgmental, critical, and would become just as negative, as the people who I perceived were responsible, for disrupting my happiness. They were who I blamed, when things weren't going my way, or when it just felt like they were getting in the way of my agenda, slowing me down, or interrupting my progress, goals, or To Do List.

The second thing I came to understand, is that it's a scientific fact, that every part of the human body, including each cell, has a "mind of its own". So, when I gained this innerstanding, I began to be mindful of 2 things: 1) Every emotion I feel and everything that I think and say, my cells are going to respond to it, for better or worse, and 2) I need to treat my body, as the most important thing in my life. I'm sure that many of you have heard that "Health is Wealth", well, this is an understatement, because without good health, we're no good to ourcellves, or anyone else. So saying no to others, no to phone calls, texts, emails, and events is my 1st line of defense. It's cellfish, but it's the lifestyle that keeps me healthy 99% of the time, and stops me from feeling overwhelmed. So, it makes sense to me, to support my body, as much as my body supports me. This obviously isn't an easy undertaking, finding time to take care of ourcellves, is a job in itself, but we must do it, because our life, peace of mind, and wellbeing truly depend on it.

The third thing that leveled up my wellness, is the practice of counting my blessings. A few years ago, during a very difficult time in my life, when I was learning more hard lessons, that I had created, and just needed a break, that break came in the form of an email, with a 30 day GRATITUDE practice, from "The Secret." It instructed me, to write down everything that I was grateful for, daily. Within a few days, I began to notice a change!!! When I'd get in bad moods, the bad mood wouldn't be as heavy, once I replaced negative thoughts, with gratitude, and if I got mad, or sad, I wouldn't stay that way, as long. I began to, much more readily, turn a negative into a positive, and with a quickness, my life got better and better. Then one day, toward the end of the 30 days, it hit me that I was feeling joyous, for no reason, in particular, and when I thought about it, I had been feeling joyous, for a few days. I felt so much joy, so often, that it felt like a surprise, like the kind that seemed too good to be true. What was interesting was, not much had actually changed in my world, externally. I already had a loving family, who I got along with (for the most part), I had the usual ups and downs in life, I was working at a job that gave me some fulfillment, although it was stressful, and not my ultimate end, but my needs and many of my wants were met. Nevertheless, prior to practicing gratitude, having so many blessings didn't stop me, from focusing on whatever negativity would pop up. No amount of sage, or removing mycellf from someone else's negative innergy, was going to fix the problem. Me. I was the problem, but when I started to focus on what was right in my life, instead of what was wrong, BAM!!! That part.

On the other side, however, I became nervous about losing this newfound feeling. So, I decided to not stop my gratitude practice, at 30 days, and began keeping a gratitude journal, as a lifestyle, so that I wouldn't lose this precious gift. Then another surprise came, after a few months of journaling, solely, about gratitude, I began to, simply, think, speak, and feel gratitude, throughout my day, without writing it down. Wala!!! I had internalized the practice, and never looked back, but it's practice that makes perfect. So, when I drift off into a bad mood, or when life happens, I go back to square one, and focus on GRATITUDE. It is this gratitude practice that has led me to share with you, how I formed a deeper relationship with my body, spending more quality time with mycellf, and becoming more mindful to listen, intently, to the body that was so graciously helping me, each and every day. My body. So, please join me, in an intimate conversation with my body, my best friend.

My Head, Neck, Mind & Brain

WOW!!!
THANK YOU for protecting one
of my greatest assets.
THANK YOU for holding up the
real camera in my life.
THANK YOU for all you remember, for
me, every second and minute of my day.
THANK YOU for helping me to learn, develop
new skills, and execute all of my daily tasks,
at home and on my job. THANK YOU for having
the power to change my painful experiences,
into powerful learning experiences. THANK
YOU for reminding me to be calm,
when I get too busy, thinking or worrying,
and give mycellf a headache.
Please forgive me, when I need
more faith, because
I truly honor and admire you, as a
divine expression of the Most High.
I am in awe, of how you remember
all my experiences, and everything
that I've seen, and heard.
I know that you are my central power station,
and that you tell the rest of my body what to
do. So, I vow to take care of you, by giving
you just what you need, to sustain yourcellf.
I honor you by giving you rest, being quiet,
being still, and allowing mycellf to just be.
I give thanks that you are the vessel, that
has great command over my life.
I can think, I can speak, and I can do.
Amen and Ase'

*"Thoughts are things, I create my life,
by what I think, say and do!!!"*

My Will

Oh will, I breathe deep to acknowledge you. You are a mighty helper, and the essence of God's liberty. I am so grateful for the gift of free will, and choice. I seek you in everything, difficult, I endeavor to do, and you come through for me, every time. THANK YOU!!! THANK YOU for being my strong tower, that works in unison with the spirit within me, we are such a strong team. I AM so grateful to be a part of our team, and the creative process that takes me to my highest heights. You're awesome and you make me feel strong. It is my iron will that gives me the feeling that I can do all things, and I do, because you exist. I honor you today, and always, for making my life possible!!!

I AM, THAT I AM

My Eyes

I see you!!! What do you see?
THANK YOU for the beautiful dance that we
do, the giving and receiving of your gift.
I humbly and gratefully receive. I care for
you, THANK YOU for giving me options,
for opening when there's something for me
to look at, and for closing when I don't want
to see, for gently closing when I want to go
deeper inside of mycellf, and for speaking
to others without ever saying a word.
THANK YOU for the tears you shed for me,
THANK YOU for bathing me, on the inside,
and for giving me a safe space, as I
SURRENDER, to your wisdom.
You cleanse me, you heal me, and set me free!!!
I greatly admire and appreciate your versatility,
and intelligence, and I seek to rest for you.
I seek to keep you well, and to use
your gift for the rest of my life!!!
Thank you for serving me, you
are precious in my sight!!!

"I once was blind, but now I see"

My Ears

"Hark, who goes there?" "Inquiring minds want to know."
A noisy world, peace and quiet, would I ever
know the other, without you beloved?
You're my special friend, and I have appreciated
you, so much, throughout the years. Seeking
answers, satisfying curiosity, allowing me too
much and not enough, all at the same time.
Nevertheless, I THANK YOU SO MUCH, for
without you, I wouldn't even recognize mycellf.
Not missing a thing, you have been my constant
companion, my partner in crime, yet, still,
we grow together, respectfully choosing to
respect others, by listening, or not listening.
What a long journey we've made, but I THANK
GOD that you are one of my greatest supporters,
and that we're navigating this terrain together.
THANK YOU KINDLY!!!

"We have two ears, and one mouth, so we can listen twice as much, as we speak"

My Nose

INHALE!!! EXHALE!!! Ahhhhhh!!!
MANY, MANY THANKS to you, for receiving
the breath of life!!! You, my dear, are a life saver!!!
I need you so much!!! I need you every second
of every day!!! You are my everything!!!
You make me feel so healthy, so strong,
so clear, so focused, and self assured!!!
I would be lost without you!!! It's so enjoyable
being with you, you make me feel so good!!!
Knowing that I have you to count
on, knowing that you're there to
comfort me, when I get stressed,
you reassure me, when life is hard, you
calm me down, and give me patience.
I trust you, because with you, I can do no wrong.
Then, the icing on the cake is that because of you,
I recognize the sweetness of life, you
help me to stop and smell the roses.
You tease me, right before I taste something
delicious, and you warn me like a homegirl,
ah ah don't you dare put that in your mouth.
You got my back!!! And I've got yours.
I blow out all the toxins, so that we can work
together, in unison, side by side and step by step.

"BREATHE DEEP, BREATHE OFTEN"

My Mouth & Tongue

My, my, my, you & I what a pair!!! Is that a foot?
A knife, I say? Nope it's that little member.
You are such a treasure chest of everything!!!
So much excitement awaits me, in
your wonderful company!!!
You make me feel so smart, while I must
watch out for you, at the same time, but...
THANK GOD for my other parts that support
us, whenever we fall short. Indeed.
We all work so well together, I
don't ever want to lose you.
THANK YOU FOR BEING MY FIERCEST
ADVOCATE, AND MY FRIENDLIEST ALLY!!!
THANK YOU for giving me one
of life's simplest pleasures.
We've been on so many journeys together,
and I couldn't make it, without you.

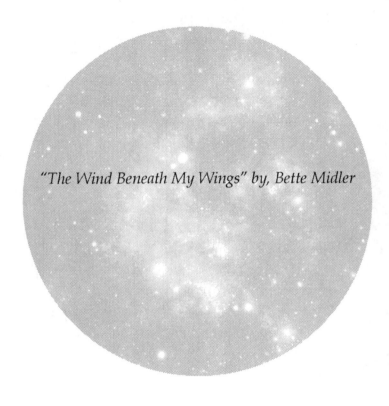

"The Wind Beneath My Wings" by, Bette Midler

My Arms & Shoulders

You romantic, loving, resourceful, strong part
of me, you make me smile!!! We want the same
things, moving like rhythm and rhyme, it's so
easy between us. Knowing, taking and giving,
before we ever have to say it. You have
bared so many burdens, for me,
yet, you stay strong, always & forever.
I rest in your presence, while sometimes,
seemingly, you're doing most of the work.
I love you, I need you, and I appreciate
you!!! I repeat, I love you, I need
you, and I appreciate you!!!
I won't take you for granted, ever again.
We're lifers!!!

I respect our reciprocal relationship

My Hands & Fingers

Holding, rubbing, scratching, typing,
writing, pointing.., you are so useful
and helpful, to say the least!!!
THANK YOU for fulfilling one of my
passions, of putting words on paper.
We've gone through a lot together,
you've put up with a lot too, and
I'm sorry that I've neglected you at
times, and haven't always helped
you to look, or feel, your best.
I THANK YOU for forgiving me,
when I fall short. I know that you
know, it's not for a lack of desire,
and that we are still in it, together. You're always
here for me, and I want you to know, that I vow
to take better care of you, to stop picking on
you, to give you as much as you give, to me, and
to show you the appreciation, that I really feel
for you. You are quite the athlete, you have so
many parts, small parts, strong parts, and your
confidence commands a standing ovation.
HIGH FIVE!!!

"I never stop reaching, I never stop loving"

My Breasts

1st PLEASE allow me to apologize!!!
I'm really sorry!!!
You weren't doing anything
wrong, it was my fault!!!
I'm so sorry, for how I used to treat you!!!
No, no, no, you were perfect how you were!!! I
just wanted to be a big girl, and look like Mom,
or magazine models. Mmm mmm
mmm remember the training bra,
with the elephant on it LOL?
I wanted to die, right then!!! I was so frustrated,
and longed to be in the women's department,
where the lace bras, with real straps,
and padding, were. Bye bye toilet
paper, hello breasts!!! I knooow.
You were just sooo flat!!! I know
I should have accepted you, as is,
deferred my gratification and all,
but I couldn't, I was like get a life!!! But, then
you came, and I was like heyyy!!! You go girl!!!
But, I know better now, sis!!! THANK
YOU for feeding my babies. THANK
YOU for creating nourishment, and being
a safe space, for loved ones who needed
to rest, in my bosom, for comfort.
You are sacred, through all our highs and lows.
Please pardon me!!!

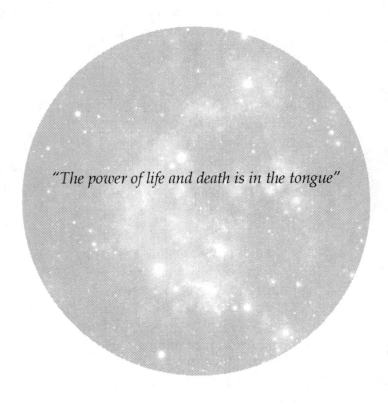

"The power of life and death is in the tongue"

My Heart

Hi Sweetheart!!! I feel you beating
inside of my chest. I hear you...
I LOVE YOU so much!!!
THANK YOU for keeping me alive!!!
THANK YOU for working for me
every day. You are the best!!! You
are so brilliant and incredible.
I'm so in awe of you, for you are
wonderfully made. I AM so grateful that
you live inside of me, and make it possible
for me to function, walk, exercise, and
live my life. Thank you for your divine
presence, and for helping me to figure out
what feels right, and what or who needs
to be in my life, or not. I appreciate your
love, I appreciate the way that you speak
to me, I appreciate the way that you help
me, to speak my truth, encouraging me to
know if I'm being as real as possible, if I'm
compromising, or taking on too much. You
have that unique way of becoming heavy
and tight, or free and light, so that I know
when I need to make a change, to help keep
us healthy, or when I'm doing just fine.
You are the best friend I ever
had. I love you so much.
I owe you my life!!!

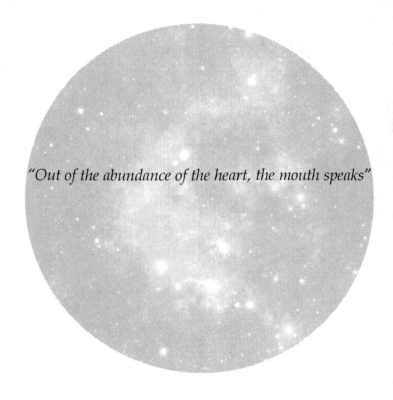

"Out of the abundance of the heart, the mouth speaks"

My Chakras

Dear chakras, you illuminate
me, you are me, invisibly.
You are so real!!!
THANK YOU for expanding my awareness,
and for allowing my senses to multiply.
Thank you for each of your purposes, and for
enabling me to go deeper into my TRUE cellf.
THANK YOU for giving me those gentle nudges,
when I'm off balance, and not doing my part.
One at a time, your existence gives me
the opportunity to grow closer,
and closer, to my divine potential. So,
THANK YOU, for you are all knowing.
You are the truth!!! You are beautiful!!!

"My chakras are open and receptive, they are balanced and aligned. They receive all divine intelligence and all divine guidance."

My Lungs

You are awesome!!! THANK YOU so much for keeping me alive, and for helping me to relax. THANK YOU so much for giving me that sense of peace, that sense of well being, and that sense that everything is alright. I love breathing with you. I love that feeling of freedom, after inhaling a long, deep, cleansing breath. I love how light I feel when you allow me to breathe, you cleanse my cells, my mind, my heart, my blood, and my being. You are my life!!! You make me want to dance!!! You make me feel sensual!!! You make me feel strong and beautiful!!! I need you in my life!!! Thank you for sticking with me, and for showing me a better way to live!!! THANK YOU for forgiving me, when I haven't used you enough, and when I created distress in my body, by smoking and disrespecting the gift that you are. I appreciate you so much. THANK YOU for replenishing me, forgiving me, and THANK YOU for your mercy!!!

I trust you, you are my guide, and I listen to you when you say, slow down!!!

My Colon

Blessed colon, THANK YOU for lightening my load, THANK YOU for loosening me up, THANK YOU for CLEANSING me. You are a miracle in itself. From the top to the bottom, from the "rooter to the tooter", you keep me well. In the bathroom, it's all me. Me and my body, me and the things I ate, me and the things I thought, me and the things I felt, just me and my maker. When I urinate and have a bowel movement (BM), I go alone. I leave my phone, books, magazines and any distractions, out of the bathroom, because I have gone in there to clean you out, on the inside. Our relationship is intense, and our daily activity is just as important as the water I drink, and the baths and showers that I take. You beloved, are the center of my universe. I eliminate and take advantage, of every opportunity you give me, and I appreciate you. Once I sit down on the toilet, to make a BM, I approach it like I'm about to do the long jump, in the Olympics, every time.

This is my own personal version of Toilet Yoga® It's as simple as this...

On days when your bowels won't move, shake it off, take a long, deep breath, inhale slowly, through your nose, and exhale slowly through your mouth, like you're blowing out a candle. Squeeze your shoulders up, and then relax your shoulders, as you bring them down, as you release any tension. Repeat this motion, until you feel relaxed. Then as you feel the pressure, of your BM start to move downward, and toward your rectum and sphincter muscle, and the warm urine flows out, take another deep breath, arch your back, as much as you can, from your lower back, all the way up, through your rib cage, feel the stretch, and then roll your shoulders back, as if you're a cobra, and then exhale. Take another deep breath, inhale, exhale, and keep moving like the cobra does to the flute.

Picture in your mind's eye, the very top of your colon, to the bottom of your colon, and picture the waste completely coming out of you. If your bowels, still, don't feel like they're moving, or they're moving slowly, continue to use your breath to assist you. Take long, slow, deep breaths, inhale, and exhale, repeatedly. Relax your shoulders, then, twist your torso to the right and to the left, again, loosening up your back. Next, move your shoulders up and down, repeatedly, and then sway from side to side, like in modern dance, thinking about how relaxed you are.

Then, take your chin down to your chest, roll your neck around clockwise, and then counterclockwise, and add your abdomen, in unison. Talk to your BM, too, thank it for getting rid of the waste and toxins in your body, encourage it to come down, let it know you're working with it, and how much you appreciate it, for making you clean, on the inside. If you've eaten something that slows down digestion, such as meat and cheese, apologize to your colon, for causing it to have to work harder, on your behalf. If you're sincere about wanting to eat better, tell your colon about any changes you want to make, on its behalf. Then, by visualizing, and being in tune with your body, "see" and feel different pockets of your colon, that are full and dense, with BM. Then, work with it. Help it. Move. Do the snake dance, on the toilet. Having a BM is all about motion and movement. Breathe!!! Keep telling your colon how much you appreciate it, and speak sincere gratitude to it, for all the work it's been putting in, since Day 1. The body temple is the master of divine intelligence, and it understands what we say to it, what we mean, and when we aren't respecting it. It is all knowing. Our colons often get a bad rap, because of the smell that's produced from BM, when we eat things that aren't nutritious, or eat the wrong combination of foods, but, all is well. Let it be, and be one with your body, "the good, the bad, and the ugly". Woop!!! There it is!!! LOL...

Good job!!! Thank you colon!!!

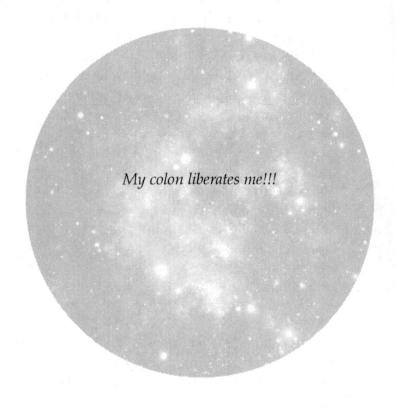

My colon liberates me!!!

My Gut/My Intuition

What is it that you want me to know?
What are you saying to me?
I owe you an apology, for all the times that
I was unfriendly, shooed you away,
and ignored you, when you knew
better. You didn't deserve that.
THANK YOU, for being patient with
me, and for loving me, even more
than I loved myself, at times.
THANK YOU for wanting the best for me, when
I didn't have the courage to change, and let go.
THANK YOU for being that reminder,
that wouldn't go away, when you'd give
me butterflies, tension, or a stomach
ache, to get me to notice you. I appreciate
you, so much, for being my coach,
and the teacher who's hard on me. THANK
YOU for encouraging me to go higher,
pushing me past the discomfort, and fear.
I HONOR YOU TODAY, AND ALWAYS.
IT'S MY MISSION AND VOW,
EACH DAY, TO TRUST YOU.

"My gut never lies"

My Organs, Blood and Systems

I just wanna take my hat off to you, and
bow before you!!! You are incredible!!!
THANK YOU for keeping it all together.
THANK YOU so much, for being so clear.
THANK YOU for the way that you speak to me,
in the affirmative, with direction, and authority.
You say what you mean, and mean what you
say. You don't play!!! When it's time to detox,
you let me know, when I've allowed anger and
fear, to get the best of me, you let me know,
and you let me know, in no uncertain terms,
when to CHANGE DIRECTION, i.e.,
ah, ah, none of that. Aaand, I have
to THANK YOU for the pain.
Your voice is important, and I hear
you. So, I submit to you, and I
honor you today, and always,
for loving me the way you do, and for the
tough love that's sometimes necessary,
as I continue to strive, to do and be my best.
You are an awesome, magnificent
reflection of God.
You are intricate, divinely intelligent,
and brilliant in purpose.
You are awe inspiring, and I
appreciate you immensely.

Thank you for the lean times and in between times, it's all good!!! You are uniquely mine!!!

My Genitalia

Hello there my friend!!! What are you
doing? Mmm hmm!!! I see!!!
Don't you just wanna walk outside
the way nature intended?
The struggle continues LOL!!!
There's so much to talk about!!!
Where do we start!!!
I remember you, when we were kids. You
looked so funny to me back then.
Remember how we used to peek around
the corner, to see if anyone was coming,
remember how exciting that was, to
look into the box of goodies?
The smell was well, like Mom would say "tart"
LOL... but I didn't care, I liked you, a lot.
I could always count on you, to make
me feel like a natural woman.
Remember Marvin Gaye LOL… You
sure have been good to me.
Girrrrl I just want you to know how proud
I am of you, you hung in there, for real.
I mean it, I'm proud of you, you
still got it goin on, too!!!
Mmm hmm!!! You know that's right!!!
Victoria Secret and Bath & Body
Works, was really good,

but now oatmeal and honey are real
nice, or a little tea tree, you know.
Got my 1 and only, now, yep, taught me
a thing or two, you're my G!!! Yep!!!
I had only heard about it, used to envy
my friends' sex lives. Mmm hmm!!!
But, it's all good in the neighborhood now.
I'm so glad we're still in touch, after all
these years!!! I was worried about you,
for a minute LOL... but you bounced back sis!!!
THANK YOU FOR NEVER QUITTING ON ME!!!

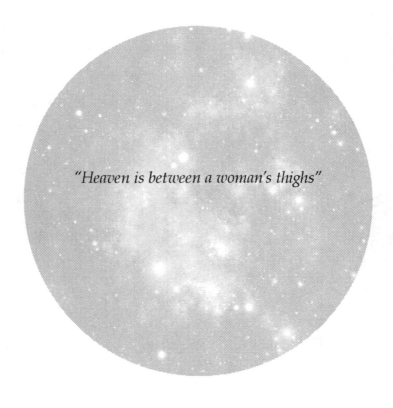

"Heaven is between a woman's thighs"

My Legs

Talk about the 2nd coming, you uhmaaze me!!!
I don't care how much we do, or how
far we go, you just keep on going!!!
You've gone from crawling and stumbling, to
climbing and leaping, and the battle scars,
don't even mention em, but it was fun wasn't it!!!
Now, you move about so wisely, systematically,
thoughtfully, and you're just so considerate of our
time, and innergy. I feel really good about you,
and having you on my team, I mean really
good!!! I, also, want to apologize to you,
for having you go places where I had no
business going, and for pushing you too hard,
when you had already told me how
you felt. I know there were a few
times, when I didn't give you
the respect that you deserve, but I'm sorry,
I really am. I know you forgive me,
because you're still here, doing a good job for us,
but I still need to say, will you please forgive me?
I just had to say it, because I don't wanna
take you for granted, ever again.
So, I'm working on things, and I
appreciate your trust, I really do!!! I
really appreciate how you work,
and how you still look, and I want
to do better for you, too.
"I'm in it to win it"!!!
THANK YOU for keeping me around!!!

"The race isn't given to the swift, or to the strong, but to the one who can endure until the end."

My Feet

Lawdy Miss Flawdie!!! Can we take a minute
to roll on the floor, and just laugh? Whew!!!
Our love/hate relationship was hilarious!!! I
don't know who was tougher, you or me,
like Cinderella's stepsister squeezing on
Mom's pumps that were 2 sizes too small,
or the blessed assurance of our ancestor's DNA,
refusing to be moved!!! You a strong sistah!!!
It's a wonder we wound up here
together, co-existing beautifully,
after all the damage that was done, yet, we won!!!
The 2 of us together, 1 too footloose and fancy
free for her own good, and the other, grounded
(i.e., you betta sit yourself down
somewhere LOL…)
THANK GOD for shea butter!!! THANK
GOD for Big Momma!!! THANK
YOU for all the highs, lows,
and anywhere in between that you
took me, to and through!!!
You have been so good to me, THANK
YOU for your immeasurable grace,
mercy, and perseverance.

"Stand Strong, Stand Firm"

THANK YOU dear Creator, for our unlimited Universe, for all its creation. THANK YOU for giving me the privilege to co-exist with you. THANK YOU to my body, for allowing me to be present with you, every day and for the blessing of 2nd and 3rd chances… THANK YOU for new beginnings, and continual growth. THANK YOU to whoever's reading my book, and for joining with me, on my journey, to reach my full potential. Be well!!! Be you!!! Stay True!!!

"The greatest of all things is love"

About the Author

Trudi Harper Hill (aka Ubuntu Ma'at aka Avtar Adi Kaur) is a student of life, and a woman of faith. She is an empath, HSP (Highly Sensitive Person), spiritual guide, writer, author, and founder of Truth Relief Healing® www.truthreliefhealing.com. Trudi has spent over 30 years researching the mind, body, spirit connection, doing intensive healing work, and is dedicated to cellf mastery. Drawing from the divine source within, Trudi courageously overcame childhood traumas, an eating disorder, clinical depression, loneliness, low self-worth, panic attacks, agoraphobia, negative thinking, and now creates practical, and personalized, healing and wellness programs, for her clients. Trudi is passionate about helping others, healing, our infinite potential, and being authentic, moment by moment, with compassion. She is an advocate, for cellf love, women, human rights, and animal rights, and encourages others to practice self care, like their lives depend on it. Trudi's greatest dream is for peace on earth, and for humanity to co-exist with nature.

Trudi resides in South Los Angeles, with her husband, is the mother of 2 suns, and has 3 cats. She injoys spending time in nature, with family, friends, and animals, practicing yoga, dancing, and writing.

Notes and Changes

Notes and Changes

Notes and Changes

Notes and Changes

Notes and Changes

Notes and Changes

Notes and Changes

Notes and Changes

Notes and Changes

Notes and Changes

Notes and Changes

Notes and Changes

Printed in the United States
by Baker & Taylor Publisher Services